A Life Full of Labels:

I waited 33 long years to meet the man of my dreams. When I got married on August 21, 2009 one day before Ramadan I and became Mrs. Lubna Humayun, it changed my life forever. I made the hardest decision of my life to leave my family and begin my life as a wife and companion to my husband. It was a sad day in my life's history, since my family was against the marriage from the onset because my husband did not have a stable job and with his underlying health issues they were concerned about my future with him, but I realized that if I didn't make a change for the better at that time then I would suffer for the rest of my life. Before marriage I was constantly ridiculed for my short comings by family members and so called "friends" which are now simply acquaintances. My husband was the first person in my life who accepted me for who I was and to him it did not matter how others perceived me. Unlike others he encouraged me to stand up for myself and be proud of who I am as an individual continuously praising me for my good deeds and hard work.

There were only five to six people at my wedding none of which were my immediate family members, but those five people made me feel wanted, loved, and secure. I fasted for the first time in 33 years the day after we got married. It was truly a life changing event. I felt pure, clean, fresh, and re-energized. It was so easy to fast for 30 days from sunrise to sunset because all I needed my whole life was a companion who needed the same things that I did. We both shared our thoughts and feelings about the meaning and message of Ramadan. For so many years I questioned why my parents didn't place importance on this Holy Month. Maybe it was because their parents didn't place importance on it either, but I didn't worry about that anymore because I knew that when I became a mother it was my job to place importance on Islam.

Label 1: Too Old to be Married and have Kids Label (Not fit to be a Mother or a Wife)

At 36, I had my first daughter and my mother's initial reaction, as she was driving her new Beamer (the car they got just after my grandfather passed away), "Are you sure?" I let that one slide, but I still cannot forget that look on her face. My initial reaction was, "My own mother does not think that I am fit to be a mother?" I was so shocked to hear her response and feel completely unwanted by the woman who gave birth to me. It was as if she thought I was incapable because she indirectly assumed that I would have challenges being a mother, but then I thought, everyone has challenges being a mother for the first time, the most important thing is that they have a support system and people who care for them, of which I had none.

It was hard, really hard I was on psychiatric medication to prevent a relapse and a month before my first born was ready to enter the world I was hospitalized. I did have a relapse after the baby shower my parents organized at their home. I saw my so called "friends." ***And*** a real friend told me, they are not your friends, they are your enemies, and now I know why she said that.

My second daughter was born at 5 pounds 5 ounces on December 31, 2014 at 12:21PM. 12-31-14 @ 12:21. My mother's reaction to number 2 was, I thought you would wait.? I didn't say anything and again just let it slide. They came to help us from Chicago as we were in Michigan and they found it easy to go back and forth every weekend to be with their "friends." This lasted for about a month until I was on my own. It was difficult but I did get. through it. But it was then that I lost my balance. I noticed at my middle daughter's first birthday that I could not regain balance. Was it the weight, was it fear of falling or was it "mental" (Agoraphobia)???... a dilemma I still struggle with to this day. According to my Psychologist Nicole Garcia and Riverside Psychiatric Medical Group Agoraphobia means you have a fear of going outside. I love going outside and I have a goal of not using a walker soon enough. There is no excuse for me not to walk again because before pregnancy I used to walk just fine. I just have a fear of falling or hurting myself and not being able to grab onto anything if I do. This to me is normal seeing that I have used the walker as a crutch or security blanket for seven years and my brain is so used to grabbing on to something for help that I "see" that as normal. It will take time but slowly I will begin to realize that my own body has enough strength and support to do just that, support itself without using any additional support.

My third daughter was our lucky charm born in California a week before we bought our first house and just before my eldest was going to start school. My mother's reaction to number three was, "Again?" "How are you going to handle it?" I thought that during each pregnancy my mom had an excuse as to why I should not have children. She was not happy at all that I was pregnant and being a mother would change me for the better. Instead she found excuses as to why she thought I was unfit to be a mother. My youngest is now 2.5 years old and I must say that I am handling everything just fine.   This is where I am now and with her, I tried nursing, but it just was not working. A friend told me that perhaps she does not like the taste of your milk." "But don't worry if she thinks it is good for her, she will take it otherwise she will not." And I thought Eshaal is already being a scientist! What Enaaya strives to be at age 7! Eshaal was already observing and exploring and experimenting and acting on what she thought was right for her. As I sit her today my three angels are so engrossed in watching a video on how to make something. I don't know what that something is but I know I will soon find out because all three will do it together and all three will achieve their lifelong dream of Finding the answer with Allah SWT (God's) guidance, support and help just as I have finally done after 43 years. I was telling my husband that day when I picked up the Quran and just started reading it that if my parents taught me how to read this at an early age, I would be a whiz kid at age 10! Maybe you will be too.!!

My two-and-a-half-year-old daughter loves to Learn. She is a Humayun Hero. As you watch this video note my probing questions to her as she identifies the letters shown. She is using her hands and fingers to manipulate the marker in a way that is comfortable to her before I show her the correct way. Notice how @ first she refuses to hold the marker correctly and she continues to model her way of writing. Despite the latter, she identifies all letters and pictures accurately. Sometimes it is hard to notice due to the video but listen closely as she names each letter correctly. Aizah is my 5.5-year-old Humayun Hero. She is learning how to Write her letters correctly with proper formation of letters with the Marker. I re-direct her as she makes mistakes to write her "P" correctly. AGAIN, if you can't see it. HEAR IT. USE YOUR SENSES BE A HUMAYUN HERO! ALL HUMANS ARE HEROES IN MY BOOK! HOOT HOOT! hashtag#writinghashtag#languagehashtag#languageteaching

https://youtu.be/L2N8muRE_wc

I lived with criticism, so I learned to condemn.

My children live with praise, so they learn to appreciate.

I lived with hostility, so I learned to fight in fear.

My children live with friendliness, so they learn to be hospitable.

I lived with ridicule, so I learned to be shy.

My children live with respect, so they learn to be polite.

I lived with shame, so I learned to feel guilty.

My children live with dignity, so they learn to be proud.

My children are tolerant, so they are patient.

I became tolerant with age, so I learned to be patient over time.

My children live with praise, so they learn to appreciate.

I praise my children, so I learned to appreciate them.

My children live with encouragement, so they are confident.

I lived with discouragement, so I learned to despair.

My children live with fairness, so they are just.

I lived with favoritism, so I faced discrimination.

My children are secure, so they are faithful.

I lived with insecurity, so I learned to be anxious.

My children live with approval, so they are learning to like themselves.

I lived with disapproval, so I learned to be apologetic.

My children live with acceptance and friendship, so they have found and continue to find love in the world.

I lived with denial, so I found stress in every situation. It took time for me to find love in this world.

My kids are my Heroes, my weaknesses are their strengths, my falls, are their rises, my cuts are their bruises, my sufferings are their experiences, my accomplishments are their successes. After every fall I somehow find the strength for Allah (SWT) to rise up again. This truth became more self-evident as I grew on the inside. I don't look the best always, *I have my ups and downs like all, but a friend told me that don't let your failures shadow your children. Don't let your mistakes bring your kids down, don't let your bruises scar your children's faces. Don't let your anger be the sign of your kids' punishments. Instead use Allah (SWT) word as your guidance and you will rise up as the rest of us fall over and over again.*

TEACHING CAREER AND ACADAMIA LABEL: CP, DISLEXIA, SLOW LEARNER WHICH LATER BECAME BI-POLAR 1 DEPRESSION

At the onset of my academic career all of my diagnoses Cerebral, Palsy, Dyslexia, Slow Learner, Bi-polar depression…. Became apparent one by one. When I was young, I let my shortcomings define me but at 43, I am Confident, I have learned to cope, and I do not let all of these "labels" define me due to my environment. I was constantly put down by my family members and peers which caused me to keep my head down, and have an extremely low self-esteem, did not talk much and just went to school to study as opposed to making friends and socializing. I was my teachers' best student the one who tried so hard but still failed on all her tests and exams. The one who completed all her homework and projects on time with flying colors. The one who participated in class even if I knew the answer was incorrect at least I gave it a shot. All my teachers loved me for This, but I still could not understand why I would get C+'s or B's in class but an A for effort. It was because all through grade school, middle school and even high school I failed all of my tests. Every single multiple -choice test I would fail however I would do amazingly well on written tests or essays. When I was a student there was a great deal of rote memorization involved in learning. Now as my eldest daughter is starting her academic career teachers teach you how to recognize the "Big Picture" in everything that you are learning.

For example, if you are learning patterns in Math recognize the pattern of making ten to answer 9+8=17. Take 1 away from the 8 and make it seven and make the 9 a ten then add 10+7=17. In math it is much easier to recognize patterns to complete addition sentences then to count on your fingers to solve a problem. I did not learn this until age 43. Now Mathematical concepts like addition, subtraction and multiplication make so much more sense just by recognizing patterns. Did teachers know this when they were teaching me? Only Allah SWT (GOD) knows. Perhaps if teachers back in the 80's knew how to teach patterns my life would not have been so difficult. Despite this I will not play the blame game like President Trump blaming China for the world's Pandemic, instead I will thank Allah for helping me realize this so that I can teach my children correctly.

Label Three: Having a Disability and Working, but Feeling like a Liability

If you have a disability and have been labeled trust me this label sticks with you like permanent glue for life until you decide to take it off. What I mean is, until you decide that you will not let these "LABELS" define you, you will not let them control you they will take over your life. When I was born in 1976 there was no law for the protection of disabled Americans. The ADA did not become a law until July 26, 1990. For the first 14 years of my life disabled Americans had no rights as citizens of this country. It has only been enforceable for 30 years. When it did become enforceable no one gave it any importance or value and in my case that is still true today.   The Government states that it has strict laws (ADA) for disabled Americans but are they truly being followed? Are they truly protected by the law if you are disabled? The ADA had no value in my case. I was working as a teacher for 12 years in Chicago before moving to California and the year I was pregnant with my first born my employer did everything they could to get rid of me. They made me do bus duty when I could barely walk down the hall and maintain my balance because I had gained so much weight I looked like an elephant, they made me lift heavy objects such as chairs even though I had notification from my doctor to not do heavy lifting. They made me escort preschoolers to the bathroom and lift them up to the toilet seat even though again I could not do any heavy lifting>… why, because that was part of my job description and basically if I could not perform my job I could leave and that is exactly what I did I left… I cried and cried I ended up in the hospital for a month before my daughter was born but they did not care. Not once did they apologize not once did, they call, not once did they send an email to see how I was doing, instead they made sure that I cashed in all my retirement money so I would never teach in Illinois again… They forced me to apply for SSI disability so I could once again be labeled as bi-polar and collect my money from the government. This is where I am today.

I receive an SSI check every month for basically the amount that I was making every month as a teacher in Illinois. It does not end there.

My husband has Crones disease and he has worked at Health Insurance companies such as Blue Cross Blue Shield, Molina and IEHP to name a few. When we were in Michigan and he was working at Blue Cross his Chrones symptoms were slowly coming back because he was stressed. The doctor suggested that he should talk to his employer about giving him a seat close to the restroom so he would not have to run to the bathroom every time he needed to use it. The employer took that negatively saw him as a liability and let him go a few weeks later. His reaction, Allah SWT, (God will show them) inshallah (God Willing). When a situation spirals out of our control, we have no choice but to leave it up to Allah, (God). Even in my husband's case the ADA did not serve any purpose to protect him. He has no control over his health, but people don't seem to realize that they only see how the individual will benefit them so that they make money. It's all about what is Green. IF you can't make enough green while you are working then the company sees you as a liability and gets rid of you. This happened to both me and my husband.

My Conclusion:
To the company, the ADA, even though it is a law it holds no value or importance. When you get a job and you have a disability the company will always find loopholes to get rid of you because they don't have the time, money, or patience to deal with you. Even as an educator in my case, teachers do not see the value and importance of the ADA and they teach our children? Do you see something wrong? The problem is companies don't tell you that they have an issue with your disability because they know it's against the law to discriminate based on a disability on the other hand the company will always find loopholes to get rid of you for other reasons, i.e. performance, attendance, or even punctuality.

Government Public Accommodations for Individuals with Disabilities:

A. Handicapped parking spots
B. Wheelchair accessible facilities
C. Ramps in public places, grocery stores, schools, malls, libraries, parks
D. Special ID cards or licenses for the disabled
E. Public transportation- buses, transit systems, trains.

Who do you see using these facilities?
Why do they use them?
What is your perception of them?
How much time does it take to use these facilities?
Are they efficient?
Isn't it easier to just drive a car?
When the non-majority use these facilities how are they perceived? Are they a minority?

Do you ask a handicapped person if a they need help?
If that person was you would you ask for help?
Does it take something like the recent natural disaster in Texas or the present COVID 19
outbreak for people to realize the importance of each and every person in this world and to
come together and help each other? I sincerely hope that these two instances make people
wake up and smell the coffee. If they don't then the people in this world have more serious
issues to deal with than I thought.

Congress and the ADA:

Progress make by ADA is under attack by Congress February 15, 2018 www.thehill.com
Read article in email. Justice delayed... justice denied.

As a future educator what would you do if you had a disabled person in your class?
How would you accommodate them?
**do not single out
Include them in everything just differentiate

Perceptions continued:

What do you do when you see someone bullying someone? Do you join the bandwagon and do
what everyone else does or do you stand up for that person? Do you do what is considered
"cool" or do you do the right thing?

Resources:

United States Department of Labor- www.dol.gov
Topics, disability resources
Equal Employment Opportunity Commission- www.eeoc.gov

Employees and applicants, discrimination type
US Department of Justice and the ADA -504 plans for student
https://www.ada.gov/
Department of Health and Human Services
https://www2.ed.gov/about/offices/list/ocr/504faq.html

Family and Home Backgrounds:

Get as much information as you can from parents about students behavior, interaction with friends, family lifestyle because many times the problems that arise with disabled students in school arise from something at home, so make sure you have open communication with parents, caregivers and extended family living with the child. And get as much information from family members as possible.

How to Communicate with parents in school:

https://www.scholastic.com/teachers/articles/teaching-content/five-keys-successful-parent-teacher-communication/

So, after all are, we truly protected under the ADA?

If yes how?
If no? why not?

What would you do as an educator to make sure that you, your students, and everyone else involved in your students' education are protected?

At 43 years of age as a mother of three, a wife, an educator, and a writer I have been affected with discrimination under the ADA my entire life and still do. The most valuable lesson I learned is that my shortcomings do not define me. I am a "normal citizen" trying to live a "normal life" in a "not so normal" world.

China Virus Label #4: Is the COVID 19 Outbreak Really China's Fault?

March 19, 2020

Dear President Trump

Right to try? Corona virus reach above 10,0000 huge success how what are statistics examples? Can you use right to try with my recommendation?

Over 22,000 deaths total. Reminds me of 9-11 world, safety, outlook on life

Need to do something now the entire world is suffering from this something must be done.

After every fall in 43 years, I have had to pick up the pieces and start from scratch over and over again with a clean slate.   At present the world is anxious about what is going to happen next. Instead of worrying about what is going to happen, worry about how you will survive today. Follow instructions, listen to what is going on, and take time for yourself to heal. Pray.   talk to God. Tell your kids that you are afraid, they will listen.   If they see you doing this as a family or as a group, they will do it too. If parents are scared and panic, kids are too. If parents are calm, relaxed, and take things as they come, the kids will do it too.

A big sign of panic is social media. Use your phone or device for its purpose, do not over kill. Instead of giving the kids your cell phone to keep them busy, talk to them, play with them, find things around the house to do with them. Make them clean, make their bed, take the clothes out for the next day, etc. Establish a routine. Make a schedule. Not just for yourself, but for everyone in your household. Doing this will keep everyone sane. It has helped me tremendously in all of my daily life skills. Most of all prayer has given me peace. Talking to Allah SWT (GOD) lets me know that someday everything will be back to normal and people will change to what they used to be like. I.e. enjoy the little things in life as my husband says, make a cup of tea for mom or dad when they wake up, have your kids make breakfast it can be as simple as putting cereal in a bowl, or making a Nutella sandwich. Although basic necessities may be difficult to find right now, go get only what you need and come home. Its. Not safe to be out for too long, my kids do not go out in the rain or close to sunset time. We believe that evil spirits, (Jinn) come during that time, so it is important to stay indoors after sunset.

Take your kids with you if you can so they can see. Themselves. What is going on. Honestly, I tell my kids everything, my mom told me. It's not worth it, but in my opinion, it is, because they need to know no matter what age they are. If you tell them in a way that has meaning and purpose to you, they will understand. Kids observe and dissolve everything they see, hear, smell, taste, and feel. They use their senses to explore and create. This is how they learn. They too need an outlet just like adults, so take them with you wherever you go don't let them stay home alone it's not safe. Anything can happen. Tell them not to talk to strangers, tell them to hold hands before crossing the street, pay attention when you are dropping your kids off to school instead of looking at your cell phone and checking a text message. It's just not safe. My daughter is in first grade and where she goes to school parents are constantly on their phones in their car, while waking…. Etc. if they don't pay attention, how will their children? Then it's the teacher's fault that the child has ADD? No 99.9% of students' academic and social problems are the result of what is going on at home. As a student I always had to deal with distractions, but in 1980, these distractions were different than now. Distractions of someone talking in class, or anxiety because of a test, or worried that I would not finish my project or homework on time because I had too much that my mom wanted me to do when I came home from school. Now the number one distraction for kids is social media. And you talk about social distancing…. ?? As I child I hated going to parties, talking to people, hanging out at a bar or going to a restaurant because I felt unwanted by everyone around me. But now, that is what everyone is missing?? Why because they need something to do and they are bored at home? No. I never take my kids out to entertain them. They are entertained at home by playing, exploring, using their resources, writing, sewing, you name it they have done it at home. Take them in the backyard, have them pick flowers, go for a walk, pretend it's raining outside, or snowing, play dress up…. Imagine, explore, create…. It's not time for boredom it's time to make a change and realize that we need to live each and every day to the fullest because we do not know as a country if we will survive the next day. Inna lilahe wa inna elahe rajeoon. (Surely, we belong to Allah, and to Him we shall return.) (2:156 of Quran).

You think COVID 19 is a China virus? Why? Who is to blame? Stop playing the blame game. Do you have evidence to back up this claim?

I am no scientist and frankly speaking I believe you have no qualities for being President of our country. I take Prozac for anxiety which according to scientists could cause hair loss in a small percentage of patients. I was researching on my phone before messaging my psychiatrist to see if I could come up with some sort of home remedy for this problem. This is what I came up with: I used Ayur Herbals Shampoo make with REETHA for Normal Hair by Amla Shikakai. I picked it up from a local Indian grocery store in our area and thought I would give it a try. After a few weeks of use it completely got rid of my dandruff and flakiness. Reetha shampoo is made from an Indian soapberry or washnut.

Sapindus mukorossi is a species of tree in the family Sapindaceae. The fruit is commonly known as Indian soapberry or washnut, and like other species in the genus Sapindus, it is called soapberry. It is also a native of Western coastal Maharashtra – Konkan, and Goa in India. Wikipedia

It is found in the temperate and tropical region and used for shampoo and detergents.
A few weeks ago, I increased my dosage from 20 mg every other day, to 20mg daily. The result was a significant amount of hair loss with increased dosage. So, yesterday I tried using the shampoo again with coconut oil conditioner and the hair loss stopped significantly in a matter of hours! This shampoo along with the daily consumption of turmeric with warm, or hot water has really made a difference.

 Furthermore, my daughter suffers from eczema. I went to Sprouts an organic farmers market in Corona, CA, where I live, and picked up a homeopathic medicine for eczema which simply has the following ingredients: () I put that on her affected areas and then used coconut oil to moisturize and hydrate her skin and the irritation and itchiness decreased significantly. I also give her turmeric and honey to relieve her itching.

These are natural home remedies that my own and my husband's family have used for generations and I firmly believe that they work.

Since the onset or perhaps before the COVID 19 outbreak there has been a great deal of anxiety in our society and all over the world. People in Pakistan are dying, India are dying the two countries of my homeland. You went to India. Did you see its people? Did you see peoples living conditions, did you see how people survive there day by day? Let me tell you something. My husband was born in Pakistan. He came here for an education and treatment of his Chrones disease when he was 18 years old, now a 50-year-old man. He has not seen his family in over 30 years. Doctors in Pakistan thought Chrones disease was hemorrhoids. My maternal grandmother suffered from joint pain that came with age, but she still kept on living with no surgeries, no treatments, absolutely no doctor visits, just home remedies. By the grace of Allah SWT (God) she lived a full, happy, healthy life. On the contrary, my paternal grand-parents came to the United states in the mid 1980's and they both saw countless number of doctors throughout their lifetime for all of their underlying health issues.

The point of me saying this is for you to realize that homeopathic, home remedies used for centuries by third-world and so called "less fortunate" countries" do work. I have witnessed this with my own eyes and through my own experiences. This, in my opinion is the future of the medical industry.

So instead of blaming China or making anti-Islamic remarks and comments maybe you should go back to the basics of what the Chinese or Muslims have contributed to society. According to the QURAN, The Holy book of Muslims, our people were great contributors of science. This includes medicine, scientific facts, basic ways of living etc., etc.

That being said, Turmeric contains a yellow-colored chemical called curcumin, which is often **used to** color foods and cosmetics. **Turmeric** is commonly **used for** conditions involving pain and inflammation, such as osteoarthritis. It is also **used for** hay fever, depression, high cholesterol, a type of liver disease, and itching. Falling hair: Reetha, coconut oil,

My proposed trial cure for COVID 19 precautionary measure: if you don't have symptoms and have not been diagnosed to try and prevent COVID 19 from entering your household you have the "right to try" this:

 To prevent cough use turmeric, honey and black pepper Today, proponents of **honey** tout its miraculous healing properties, claiming that it can prevent cancer and heart disease, reduce ulcers, ease digestive problems, regulate blood sugar, soothe coughs and sore throats, and increase athletic performance.

To prevent Shortness of breath, use a steam treatment: Boil water and cover it with a towel or cloth and put your face inside to get the steam or go in the tub let hot water run and breathe the hot water.

In addition to turmeric with honey and black pepper you can try onion seeds with honey as well to prevent cough, it is said that onion seeds have a cure for everything except death.

 These are just precautionary measures and my recommendations based on homeopathic medicines used around the world as precautionary measures to prevent the spread of the virus.

These are the secrets that I hear when I am talking in my sleep, and I wanted to share them with you. I wanted to take a chance because just like you and everyone else I am scared, I am just a normal citizen, good Samaritan, women, mother, sister, wife and companion who is trying to make a change for the better.

Please take these recommendations under serious consideration as you try your best to lead the world to a better place.

Regards,
Lubna Humayun
lubna.humayun@yahoo.com
H: 951-339-8837
C: 224-735-1427
Residence: 856 Autumn Lane
Corona, CA 92881

Label #5: Being Bhori Muslim

My cursor is sitting at the top of this page…. Wasting time…. Am I having racing thoughts? Is my mind wandering? Yes, no maybe so but all I know is that if President Trump continues to play the blame game who am I to stop him because I will too. Who's to blame if my parents won't tell their siblings that I am a part of this family. I was brought into this world by Akbari's raised by them put through college by them but then at 33, when my life began, I married a Humayun and my grandmother said at first sight….. Pathanay Sunni Loog khiya, Khiya kartha…..(I don't know what Sunni people do), I was like WTF…. Pathanay Bhori loog khia Khia kartha…..my response: (I don't know what Bhori people do?). These are two different sects of Muslims that practice Islam. For years I questioned why Bohri Muslims do the things they do and what sets them apart form other Muslims sects who follow Islam. I never understood their logic for the way they do things, and I always had doubts in my mind as to why they are different. 24.1% of the world's population is Muslim. From that 24.1% less then five percent are Bhori Muslims. So that means about .4% are Bhori's. Why? What makes them special? Who is to say they are practicing Islam correctly and other sects are practicing incorrectly?

From what I remember Bhori's make up less than 5% of the Muslims in the world, but just like Dr. Dyslva, my pediatrician said when I first met her, I think Sunni is the right way... I agree because it makes perfect sense to me. I never understood what Bhori's do to this day and neither do any of my family members because when I ask them you know what they say, go ask your Dadi or Dada (Grand-mother or Grand-father) who are no longer here... so now what am I supposed to do who should I ask, Ask Allah SWT to guide you ask him for forgiveness, ask Him if you want to repent for your sins... Ask him to grant you Peace, Prosperity and Happiness, ask Him for Help. Ask no one for help but Him. He will guide you to the straight path and it is He who will tell you not to blame, who is to blame.... Yourself, maybe I don't know, only Allah (SWT) knows. Because only he is All-knowing.

I was born into Bohrisim: Being Bohri is different from being Sunni or SHIA Muslim, you ask why and I say I don't know and I really don't have an answer as to why we are so different the same questions that you have I have had for 33 years I kept asking my parents and they told me to ask my grand-parents who really did not know much about being Bohri either to be honest. All I knew is that we were "different", but I had no idea why? When I got married eleven years ago, I found the answer because my husband met a Bohri women who knew all the insides of this sect and this is what she said. (paraphrased in my own words of course and at the end I did a bit of research, which all of you who read this that are in fact Bohri will be shocked to know.

What is Bohrism in Islam?

According to unnamed sources, Bhoris's are Muslims who follow the imam Syedna Mohammad Burhannadeen Various questions arise Who exactly is Syedna Mohammad Burhanudeen? Where did he come from? How did he start Borism? What is Being Bohri? However various sources tell me that this is a completely made up and fake denomination of Islam that has made significant changes to Islamic salaaat, procedures and religious beliefs. Nowhere in the Holy Quran is it written about Bohris or their religion we are all the same and we should all unite in our similarities and making changes to Islam just because of an Islamic sect that does not exist. The actual definition of a Bohri according to Google is Gold: One Tola or **Bori** or Vori is equivalent to 11.66 grams. We know that the Nisab threshold for **gold** is 87.48 grams, so this is be equivalent to 7.2 Tolas, Voris or Bhoris.Mar 13, 2011

Label #6: Misconceptions about Islam
The Truth about Islam and Charity

If you have the intention of giving money to the poor you should do it right away. Don't wait to ask your husband or someone else in your family. Just do it if you feel the person needs help and is deserving of some money. If you say I cannot because I worked hard for this money and other people should do the same, this is Shaataan, (the devil). talking to you and telling you not to help. Rizq, (fortune) is from Allah (SWT) it is not from your hard work, it's by the Grace of

Allah (SWT) that you have been blessed with good fortune. Hypocrisy is Shaataan. In turn, when you have money in abundance you should help others, not keep it to yourself and keep wanting more: Greed. What good is your money if you cannot help anyone with it? What good is your money if others cannot benefit from your fortune? If you continue to save and not give to others or you wait until death to remember others, it is too late. So, let others benefit from you now, not later.

ISLAM AND DOLAAT (WEALTH)

Allah SWT says that if you are blessed with wealth then use it wisely. You can save money, however if you keep saving and don't spend it to help the poor or your family it is haram (forbidden by Islamic Law). Similarly, if you use your money to purchase items that are forbidden in Islam such as alcohol, non kosher food, or useless necessities or items such as travel, simple pleasures, or parties not involving family then your wealth is also haram. (Forbidden).

Consequently, if your wealth is hard earned money and you spend it on your family for clothes, food, and simple pleasures involving family or helping the poor and less fortunate then your wealth is considered halal or kosher.

In my family meaning my kids and my husband we don't have much but what we do have we cherish. We have much love in our house and with that love comes respect, honor, and dignity. We teach our children these morals essential for a well- balanced life and hope that they can one day be successful and independent. When we earn our wealth with hard work our children know it because they have watched us struggle to get what we have. They already know at such a young age, that their parents hard work for a decent living is the reason they are what they are.

In my opinion the earlier children realize that their family's hard earned halal income is feeding them, clothing them, providing them shelter and the basic needs to live a good life, the sooner they will start to learn the value of money and what it can do not only for themselves but for others as well.

It is not by choice that we are struggling but rather we have no choice but to struggle. With each struggle comes strength and with strength comes the firm belief that someone somewhere is watching over us; that someone is All-Knowing Allah SWT. It is the experience of these struggles that we become Heroes in our own unique way and are guided to the straight path of the journey of life.

وَقُلْنَا يٰٓاٰدَمُ اسْكُنْ اَنْتَ وَزَوْجُكَ الْجَنَّةَ وَكُلَا مِنْهَا رَغَدًا حَيْثُ شِئْتُمَا وَلَا تَقْرَبَا هٰذِهِ الشَّجَرَةَ فَتَكُوْنَا مِنَ الظّٰلِمِيْنَ ۝

فَاَزَلَّهُمَا الشَّيْطٰنُ عَنْهَا فَاَخْرَجَهُمَا مِمَّا كَانَا فِيْهِ ۖ وَقُلْنَا اهْبِطُوْا بَعْضُكُمْ لِبَعْضٍ عَدُوٌّ ۚ وَلَكُمْ فِي الْاَرْضِ مُسْتَقَرٌّ وَّمَتَاعٌ اِلٰى حِيْنٍ ۝

فَتَلَقّٰٓى اٰدَمُ مِنْ رَّبِّهٖ كَلِمٰتٍ فَتَابَ عَلَيْهِ ۚ اِنَّهٗ هُوَ التَّوَّابُ الرَّحِيْمُ ۝

قُلْنَا اهْبِطُوْا مِنْهَا جَمِيْعًا ۚ فَاِمَّا يَاْتِيَنَّكُمْ مِّنِّيْ هُدًى فَمَنْ تَبِعَ هُدَايَ فَلَا خَوْفٌ عَلَيْهِمْ وَلَا هُمْ يَحْزَنُوْنَ ۝

وَالَّذِيْنَ كَفَرُوْا وَكَذَّبُوْا بِاٰيٰتِنَآ اُولٰٓئِكَ اَصْحٰبُ النَّارِ ۖ هُمْ فِيْهَا خٰلِدُوْنَ ۝

يٰبَنِيْٓ اِسْرَآئِيْلَ اذْكُرُوْا

Label #Why Wander

My mind wanders at times, but my kids keep me grounded, they tell me what's real and keep me in my reality. My family is what keeps me focused every single day. I have a daily routine and I stick to it like glue, I have structure and it works for all of us. I feel if I did not have a family to take care of and show me my reality I would be in a "Nut House." The latter is exactly how I felt living with my parents for 33 years. I felt as if I was imprisoned and had no way out. I would always get to the point where my brain would set on fire with a trillion racing thoughts in my head, I would drive myself crazy then run to the doctor who would increase my medication and pretty much make me feel like a zombie who would do nothing but daydream and sleep all day and night long. This vicious cycle kept happening for 11 long years. Presently I am in California with my family and my job as a wife, a mother, an educator and a companion is to ENJOY my life with my family. We pray, we eat, we sleep, we work, we exercise, we watch TV we exercise, we play board games, we play card games, we talk, we fight, we pray even more, we have FUN together, in the same house, at the same time. This is my reality now. This is what is going to make my future brighter and better every single day from this day fourth. I enjoy explaining my struggles to others in a positive light so they can take heed. Perhaps others may be suffering from the same things that I am but in a different manner. This is the purpose of my book to inform individuals of my personal experiences and teach everyone what is right from my own shortfalls, mistakes, and "issues" if you will. A friend told me that everyone has issues they just have different ways of dealing with them. Some people stay up until the wee hours of the morning, pretending to do what needs to be done but in reality, not doing anything at all. They are just plain thinking, thinking and thinking even more until finally they can't take it anymore! Maybe they can with Allah SWT's guidance and support like I have to for the past ten years. Thanks to my husband and his family I have learned how to talk to Allah SWT and ask for help. For I believe He is listening, and He is watching over me. I do have a "Fear" of doing wrong for Allah SWT I have a "Fear" that if I do wrong for Allah SWT then I will "Pay the Price" on the Day of Judgement. This is my and my inner fear that keeps me on the straight path and keeps me going, going gone until one day I am once again a tiny grain of sand. inna lillahe wa inna elayhe rajeoon.

Label#6 : MYSTERIES OF TURMERIC TURNED INTO DISCOVERY

Going back to my roots the past two weeks, (onset of global COVID 19 Outbreak) I discovered Nature's Best Kept Secret (ReshmaBeauty.com) right in my kitchen. Turmeric. In India and Pakistan Turmeric is used to bring a fresh glow to skin before your wedding day. We put it on as a paste on the skin then take a shower. I cannot really do that on a daily basis, so I decided to drink it either in the morning with warm water and honey, or at night with warm milk. Just take one teaspoon of turmeric powder, mix it with one glass of warm water and gulp it down. Make sure you drink it all and in a matter of minutes your digestion will improve. In the same way if you put one teaspoon of turmeric in warm milk and drink it before bed, you will wake up refreshed and re-energized and feel like you have lost a considerable amount of weight. I am not a scientist, so I do not have the scientific knowledge of how this works; but give it a shot and see how you feel. I Remember, if you do not like the taste add some honey to make it sweeter.

As I mentioned earlier, Turmeric is used in Middle Eastern and Asian cooking and also for a variety of home remedies in Asian culture, particularly Indian and Pakistani Cultures. It provides a natural glow to the skin to give a bride a fresh, young look. It is used as a medicine to help treat depression, asthma, and various types of cancer. Some people may say don't believe everything you read on the internet, but based on my own experience and advice from my doctors, I can safely say that after about 2 months of continuously adding turmeric to my diet I have noticed a significant difference in my appearance, attitude, and weight. I feel much more confident, cool, calm, and collected in ways that I cannot even put in words.

I was diagnosed with Bi-polar. depression at age 22, after a six-month study abroad program in Normandy, France through my undergraduate college. Since then I have been on medicines like Depakote, Trileptal, Zoloft, Klonopin, and many others all of which made me feel like a zombie and pretty much just put me to sleep at the end of the day. At that time in my life I did not realize the affects that these medications had on my body but certainly after becoming a mother I know my body better than ever before. I know in my heart that too much of these medications can be harmful and anything in moderation is good.

Presently, coupled with a daily dose of turmeric and my current anti-depressants I feel more alive at 43 than I did at 22. My trick: In addition to adding turmeric to pancakes, I add it to my premier protein shake and drink a glass before bed. Turmeric is known to heat the body so be cautious of your intake, but it aids with digestion and weight-loss as well. If taken properly it can benefit you a great deal. In my previous posts I have shown you how to add it to breakfast but today I will tell you how to add it to my protein shake. Note to self: Make sure you drink this on an empty stomach either when you wake up in the morning or at night before bed. All I did was fill my cup up with about 1\4 cup of whole milk, then fill up to the brim with hot water. Take your premier protein shake and add about 3-4 tablespoons of Premier Protein (I used chocolate), if you add the protein shake there is no need to add sugar to the drink. It goes down easier with a tiny bit of sweetness from the protein shake; honey has the same affect. Stir the mixture together and just gulp it down. Wait about 30-45 minutes and you will feel sleepy and want to go to bed. The next morning when you wake up you will feel refreshed and energized and maybe even feel like you have lost a few pounds. If you drink it in the morning then it will not have the same affect; as at night, but it still helps with digestion throughout the day. Try this regimen for a month and you will be amazed at the results.

Ingredients

The Golden Milk Humayun Style

Label #6: Mysteries of Turmeric Continued.

 So far, the doctors I have spoken with do not have any scientific knowledge of how Turmeric works and in my opinion that is why it is a mystery. All I know is that it has anti-inflammatory prosperities which make it beneficial for digestion. It also warms the stomach and can cause kidney stones if not taken properly. If you have any doubts consult your physician before intake. It has been used in Asian cultures for generations to aid prevention s of depression, asthma, and cancer according to various anecdotal records of Asian cultures. It is also used quite a bit in Pakistani and Indian cooking.

Yesterday I thought I would try something new with this mystery ingredient, Turmeric with Protein Water. All I did was mix one teaspoon of Turmeric in Premier Protein water and drank it warm. The Protein water is Peach flavored and naturally sweet so there is no need to add more sugar , it goes down easy. Below is what it looks like:

Premier Protein Water

Ingredients

*Label #7: Home Remedies: Different Uses of Coconut Oil
and Reetha Shampoo*

As mentioned in my previous post entitled Benefits of Reetha, I used coconut oil to moisturize my feet. My 7.5-year-old daughter suffers from Eczema which makes her skin really dry. Along with a homeopathic medication for eczema I use coconut oil for moisturizing her entire body. Its concentrated and thick formula provides enough hydration to last the day. Whereas a normal lotion such as Nivea or Aveeno may not have the same results. A few weeks ago, I noticed my hands were getting dry due to constant washing of dishes with warm or hot water. I decided to try coconut oil on my hands after washing them. What happened? My hands regained their moisture after 3 days of continuous use and at 43 I still look like 22! Furthermore, Sometimes, during my menstrual cycle, my vaginal area gets dry, so I put coconut oil on it to relieve dryness and find the same results as mentioned above.   In Pakistan and perhaps in India as well, mothers put coconut oil in children's hair for moisture, luster, and strength, in turn it makes their hair grow faster, softer, and smoother. I put it in all three of my daughters' hair for two weeks and have already noticed a significant difference. In fact, I also use it in my own hair. This is a great way to get natural wavy curly hair without putting chemicals of various shampoos in your hair. Using natural products made by our environment does make a difference. Once again Reshma Beauty and I validate their claim of Nature's Best Kept Secrets.

Don't forget to purchase homeopathic medication for Nail Fungus from Sprouts Farmers Market. This is what I used to medicate my nails and now after continued use my nails are getting softer, healthier, and easier to cut. In addition to the Nail Fungus medication, I use Quantum Health Athlete's Foot, Quick Drying Anti-Fungal Formula. It has a unique blend of herbs, vitamins, and other topicals that help ease and stop burning and itching on the affected area.

You can also use Reetha Shampoo as detergent which is its original purpose in India as mentioned in previous post. This is what I did. I put 2-4 droplets of Reetha Shampoo in my detergent (you can use any detergent for this), mixed it with my finger and put it in the washer. As the washer was washing the clothes thick suds appeared and the smell of the clothes was like fresh flowers. Absolutely refreshing. Take a look at my previous post to find out where you can get this amazing product that can be used for hair, skin, and clothing.

I mentioned Reetha Shampoo and the benefits it had on my dry scalp and flakiness. Since it has drastically and almost completely gotten rid of my dandruff. I thought I may be able to use it on other parts of my body as well. I suffer from dry skin on my feet and nail fungus. I used Reetha shampoo to wash my feet. My guess is, that since the product is very concentrated, I can use a little bit and it will go a long way. Based on personal experience I have used this shampoo to wash my feet for about 3 weeks now and the irritation is slowly healing. Along with Reetha I put coconut oil on my feet to moisturize it. This daily ritual makes my feet feel softer, lighter, and more refreshed. I noticed that if I put socks on after moisturizing with coconut oil my feet feel sweaty, and this causes itchiness. As a result, I only wear socks when necessary, otherwise wear crocs in the house. This lets my feet "breathe." My recommendation is that if you have dry skin on your feet, or fungus but do not have insurance or money to see a doctor, try this daily practice and see what happens.

This excerpt is based on personal experience of using these products and they do work for me, so why not give it a shot. After all, in my opinion natural home remedies for common health problems along with household use, are the future of medicine and part of Nature's Best Kept Secrets./https://reshmabeauty.com/

Label 8: Creative uses of Protein

Wow !!I guess my creative juices are flowing. Today I decided to make another protein powered brunch called Protein Packed French Toast. It's just like the pancake but with a simple little twist. Here we go:

April 10, 2020

Ingredients:

1.   Four Eggs
2.   1\4 cup Premier Protein Shake- I used chocolate
3.   Honey put as desired for sweetness
4.   1 baby teaspoon of turmeric
5.   Gopi Cow Ghee (Clarified Butter from Cows)

Add all the ingredients in a bowl whisk together until smooth texture
**Tip if you are in a rush in the morning let the mixture sit in the fridge the night before and prepare the final product in the morning. Otherwise if you have time prepare the mixture and the dish in the morning. Below is what the mixture should look like.

Protein Packed French Toast Mixture

Gopi Cow Ghee (Clarified Butter from Cows)

Melted Butter in Frying Pan

Dipped Bread in Mixture

Bread in Frying Pan

Fully Cooked Protein Packed French Toast

Yummy!

My kids loved it with whipped cream and so did I, but my husband enjoyed it with Maple Syrup and Chai. Finally, something my whole family loves to eat**! Success! I am a Humayun Hero!**

�

 According to Sheila Clarke, my Nutritionist at Riverside Medical Clinic in Riverside, CA, you should start your day with protein as it does not stay in your body. My hypothesis is that the more protein you eat or drink not only in the morning but throughout the day the more weight you will loose. Take caution, too much protein is not good and if you have questions consult a doctor. I am simply telling you what works for me, but what works for some may not work for others. According to Dr. Martin Perez, Bariatric Surgeon at Riverside Medical Clinic, if you want to lose weight quicker than your normal pace you can have more protein. He advised me to have another protein shake at lunchtime but that sounded a little boring to me. My daily breakfast usually consisted of Premiere Protein Shake which has 30 grams of protein and only one gram of sugar with only 160 calories or Clear Premier protein water with 20 grams of protein which is a little too concentrated for me so I add a little fresh fruit and dilute it a bit to get my desired consistency. When I am really hungry in the morning, I have a Premier Protein Bar with 30 grams of protein but 260 calories. I was getting bored with this breakfast so this morning I decided to add a little twist to my normal protein shake and make what I call a Protein Packed Pancake. It looks like this:

Protein Packed Pancake Final Product

These are the ingredients:

1. Pancake mix of your choice
2. Steel cut oats- I used Quaker steel cut oats
3. Premier Protein Shake any flavor - I used chocolate
4. Honey

First add desired amount of pancake mix and steel cut oats to a bowl make sure that steel cut oats are less than the amount of pancake mix. The oats add texture to the pancake while the pancake mix forms the pancake. Then slowly add protein shake to dry ingredients until you have reached your desired consistency and all of the pancake mix is dissolved in the shake. Finally add about 2-3 teaspoons of honey for a little sweeter kick. Below are some pictures of the process for you to see:

Premier
Protein
30g PROTEIN
160
1g
24
LOW FAT
NO ARTIFICIAL GROWTH HORMONES
Chocolate
11 FL OZ (325 mL)

Protein Pancake in a Pan

Protein Pancake from one side

You can add a little creamy whipped cream on top or I dipped it in what we call Malai its a creamy milk spread made from milk fat. I did not eat too much of that, but it REALLY TASTES GOOD with a little cream. This breakfast is wholesome, filling, and nutritious at the same time. It keeps you full throughout the morning and the best thing is, you don't feel guilty after eating it because if you ate 3-4 regular pancakes from IHOP or at home, that may be four times the sugar and calories! So, give it a try and see what you think!

Malai

Protein Packed Yogurt with Protein Packed Coffee

. Ready for yet another one of my favorite breakfast creations?! Well I am. The ingredients are simple. Chobani Strawberry yogurt, Cream of Wheat and about 1\4 cup of Premier Protein Shake (I used chocolate). Here is a picture of the ingredients:

Ingredients

Just put a small portion of yogurt in a bowl mixed with about a fist full of cream of wheat mix together then add the protein shake as much as desired. For a thicker consistency add more cream of wheat. The cream of wheat does not have to be cooked it can just be added to the yogurt for more energy. It's a great source of Iron and calcium that keeps you full throughout the morning.

Another option for a light breakfast with a kick is Protein Packed coffee. Just pour the protein shake in a coffee cup heat for 1 min and 45 seconds in microwave and add one teaspoon of coffee stir well. This is what it looks like.

Protein Packed Coffee

Now you can drink coffee without feeling guilty. No added sugar or sweeteners just protein and coffee. Much healthier than any energy drink I have ever had. Go ahead and give your morning a great start.

These healthier options take the boredom away from eating just plain old protein in the morning. As Sheila Clarke says, "I tell my clients that their breakfast does not have to be boring, so don't make it that way, try something different and new and you will find yourself happier and more energetic even before you start your day.

ULTIMATE LABEL#9:TURNED INTO DISCOVERY: 2020 IS GOING TO BE THE YEAR WHEN I GET MY LIFE BACK IN ORDER AND GO BACK TO WORK

Two out of my three children will be attending school in the fall of 2020, that means it's time for me to start thinking about what I want to do for the rest of my life. Honestly my husband's work situation is very unstable due to his health conditions so just in case something happens to him I need to be prepared and try to live my life on my own two feet. I have a solid education and now I am used to my motherly responsibilities, so even if I find part-time work for the time being it will be okay since I do not want to lose my SSI benefits right away. I plan on re-vamping my resume and using my skills to highlight my strengths and accomplishments as a teacher, mother, wife and "normal Human" trying to be successful and attain my American dream in this world. I want to make sure my children have a secure and bright future and for that I need to stand on my own two feet and become independent. I will turn my weaknesses into fears for Allah SWT and in turn those fears will be my biggest accomplishments in the very near future. I do not want my children to suffer the same way that I did so for that I sincerely need to make some serious sacrifices and realize that my wrongs could, and will be, their rights. They too have a right to an education and equality in the workplace, and a life free from hate or bullying, they too have a right to peace, prosperity and purpose.   After all they are the Humans that I raised and gave birth to, so they too like every other Human on this earth have a right to be HU-MaY-Uns…. (Humans).

____

ⁱ